And lifting up His hands
He blessed them.

For Sawyer, Annabelle, Lydia, Flynn, Henry,
Felicity, Oliver, and Evangeline with much love

Concordia
Publishing House

Founded in 1869 as the publishing arm of The Lutheran Church—
Missouri Synod, Concordia Publishing House gives all glory to God
for the blessing of 150 years of opportunities to provide resources that
are faithful to the Holy Scriptures and the Lutheran Confessions.

Published 2019 by Concordia Publishing House
3558 S. Jefferson Avenue, St. Louis, MO 63118-3968
1-800-325-3040 · www.cph.org

Illustrations © 2019 Concordia Publishing House
Text © 2019 William Chancellor Weedon

Manufactured in Shenzhen, China/055760/300690

1   2   3   4   5   6   7   8   9   10   28   27   26   25   24   23   22   21   20   19

See My Savior's Hands

Written by William Chancellor Weedon
Illustrated by Martin Hargreaves

CONCORDIA PUBLISHING HOUSE • SAINT LOUIS

Have you ever followed the hands of Jesus?

See them as Mary first held Him—His tiny hand wrapped around a finger as He snuggled in the warmth of her hug.

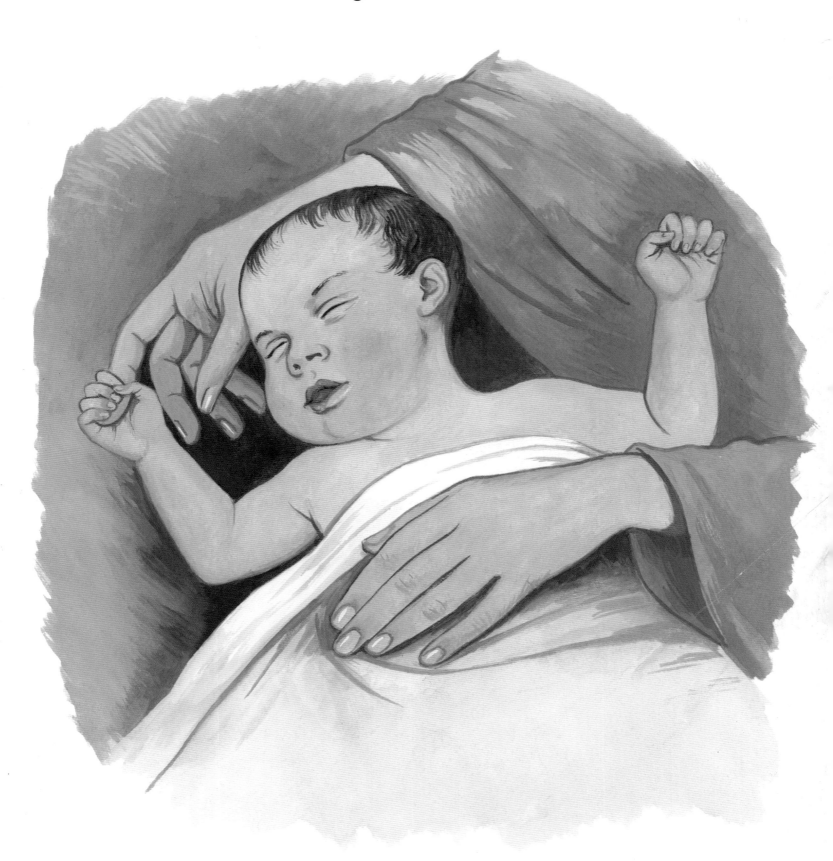

See His hands as He touches the white beard of old Simeon at the temple.

See His hands as He learns to smooth the wood and help Joseph in the carpenter shop, hands becoming rough even as a boy.

See His hands as He opens the Torah and reads from it, a finger following along with the words.

See His hands as they fold when John puts Him beneath the waters of the Jordan River.

See His hands as He touches the leper and the leprosy disappears at His words: "Be clean!"

See His hands as He receives the loaves and the fish and blesses His Father for His goodness.

See His hands as He pats the donkey's head, riding into His holy city.

See His hands taking a towel as He stoops to wash dirty feet and dry them, one by one.

See His hands as He takes bread into them, as He blesses and breaks and gives His body.

See His hands as they hold the cup and He offers the sacrifice of thanksgiving, His own blood.

See His hands outstretched in the garden,
trembling as He prays to the Father,
"Not My will, but Yours."

See His hands as He touches the man and heals his ear.

See His hands at His side, not raised to defend
Himself against the blows, the spit, the hatred.

See His hands spread out against the wood, held there by nails, determined to do this for you and for your forgiveness.

See His hands writhing in agony as the sky darkens and He is left alone with the burden of all your sin.

See His hands lifeless and torn, touched by His mother as His body rests in her loving embrace.

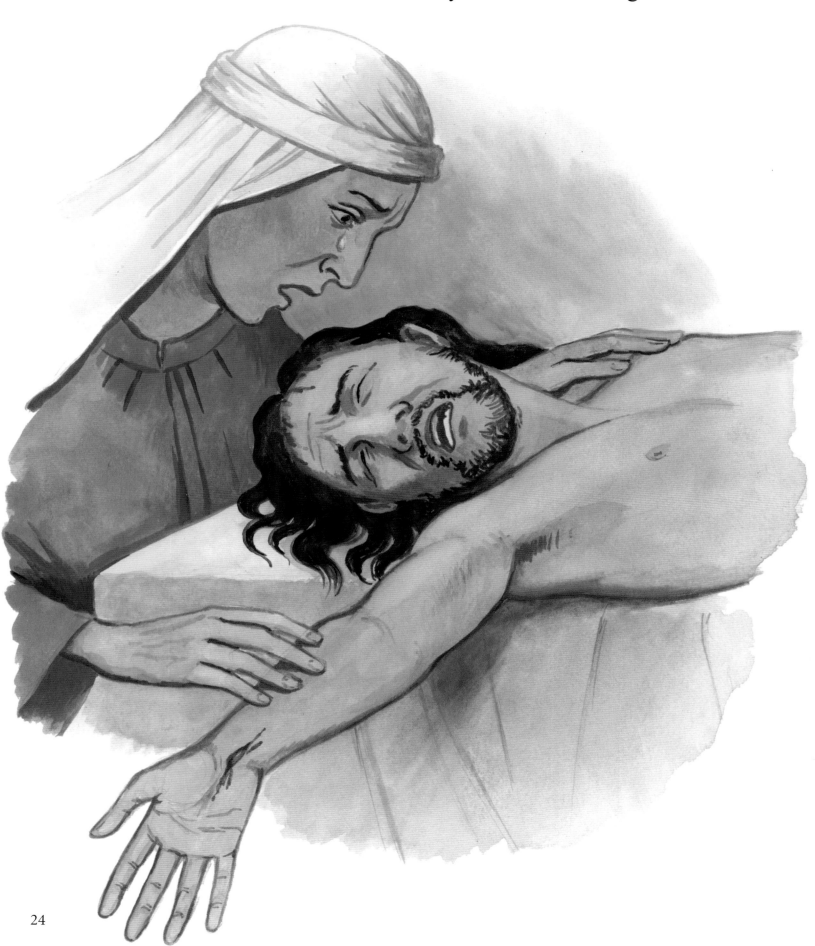

See His hands folded across
His chest, laid in a tomb, at rest.

See His hands, scars still there, yet alive again,
never to die again, reaching out to the disciples,
giving them peace, calling them to life.

See His hands preparing the fish for an early morning breakfast beside Galilee.

See His hands raised in blessing as He returns to heaven.
His hands. Your Lord's hands. Your God's hands.

And lifting up His hands, He blessed them, and for Your blessing hands, we bless You, O Lord!